Unsuccessfully Single
Sure-Fire Ways to Sabotage Your Single Life

Unsuccessfully Single:
Sure-Fire Ways to Sabotage Your Single Life

Written by Kellen Brooks
Edited by Marcus Cylar

Unsuccessfully Single: Sure-Fire Ways to Sabotage Your Single Life.

First Printing: 2016

ISBN: 978-0692709962

Ordering Information:
To purchase more paperback copies, e-books, and audio versions of the book, or for details on special discounts available on bulk purchases by corporations, associations, educators, and others, please contact the publisher at KellenBrooks.com or UnsuccessfullySingle.com.

Dedication

This book is dedicated to my maternal and paternal grandparents, who combine for over 100 years of marriage! You all have modeled successful marriage for so many others and me. You're marital success is rare and I thank you for your example.

I also owe special thanks to my mother, family, and friends who listened to the ideas for this book and encouraged me towards its completion. Your support is invaluable!

Contents

Before You Read...

I believe you are in for an exciting ride as you read through this short yet power-packed book! But before you read, there are few things you should know. This book (with the exception of what you're reading now, the foreword, and the appendices) is written as satire. My goal is to expose the absurdity of conventional dating practices, ranging from moderate to extreme, hence the writing style. The names of the individuals are completely fictional, but the stories are real.

Each section presents a concept that would pose a threat to a healthy single life and should be viewed as things you **should not** do concerning your single life and dating relationships. I invite you to come up with your own dating tips in addition to what I have provided. I also encourage you to wrestle with, question and even disagree with the content provided. Join the conversation at **UnsuccessfullySingle.com** and let's grow together in our walk as singles. Enjoy the read!

Foreword

I am honored to offer the following words as an introductory statement to this hilarious journal of anecdotes by Kellen Brooks. This comedic satirical collection of funny but serious antics is an excellent depiction of some of the challenges currently facing many singles. As long as I have known Kellen, I have known him to possess a genuinely pure heart toward every aspect of life.

His reputation for practicing honesty, integrity and godly character are a few of his most notable traits. Kellen is an enterprising millennial on the move for God and exudes a positive outlook for the future state of the church and society as a whole. I consider it a privilege to witness the leadership, stewardship and kingdom citizenship displayed in the life of this man of valor.

I am often asked for tips on the secrets behind having a successful marriage, and my reply is simple. I reply that after close to 29 years of marriage, we have agreed to remain "newlyweds". My wife Eva and I met 35 years ago, and God has blessed us to maintain a strong, Christ-centered marriage. We both concur that being "whole" as singles is the reason for much of our success, meaning that while we were single, we allowed God to make us whole before pursuing marriage.

By the grace of God, we defied the social norms of "dating and mating", which was a common practice of our times, and decided to follow a biblical path to the altar. Nothing short of outstanding favor and blessings have followed the decision we made while we were single college students living on the campus of Michigan State University.

Being single is often classified as a "life challenge" to be overcome. Particularly within the church community, being single has arguably become an undesirable state of being. Social and cultural norms in most Christian circles paint a dismal picture of singlehood that instigates an urgency to get married at all costs or by any means necessary. It has seemingly become as if marriage alone is the answer to all unanswered questions. The concept of singlehood being a time of preparation before marriage has become a novel idea.

While I agree with standards derived from scripture proclaiming marriage as "honorable", I also ascribe to the idea that being married requires some intentional work. Some of that work must be executed individually and before marriage, while other details can be worked on over time, after the vows are exchanged. God likens marriage to the relationship between Christ and the Church. This infers that there is a spiritual dynamic to both the preparation and the performance part of being married.

The state of singlehood is a great place to work on individual character issues and work out the glitches created by false expectations. These falsehoods are a recipe for being, as referenced in this book, *Unsuccessfully Single*. Kellen does an excellent job exposing the pitfalls of trying to live by the conventional views of dating and being single. This book captures the honest truth about misinformed singlehood. I have no doubt that readers will be edu-tained by this well-written book. Enjoy!

Tarence E. Lauchie', MA, CBC
Senior Pastor
Grace for the Nations Church of God in Christ
Grand Rapids, Michigan

Introduction

We were nestled in a room with a loft bed set and a nineteen-inch color TV underneath it. It was a TV set from our old house. You know, the ones with the knobs where you have to manually change the channel? You don't? I guess that means I'm getting old!

At midnight, my siblings and I (all seven of us) would crowd in that room and gather in front of that fuzzy-screened, wood-paneled television to watch a series of dating shows.

Change of Heart
Blind Date
elimiDATE

The storyline of the night was quick hook ups, sudden breakups, and hypersexuality. This was hardly a place to learn how to have meaningful relationships and garner tips to thrive as a single person. Little did I perceive how I was being negatively influenced and how this would affect my own journey of dating and singleness. In short, these shows and many others like them give us examples of how to sabotage our single life.

Singleness is that period of time before a person gets married, including one's solo time of dating no one, and then on to casual dating, committed dating, courtship, and engagement. In other words, if you aren't married, you are single.

Television and the dating practices of a family member were my *go-to* sources on how to be *Unsuccessfully Single*. From dating shows to romance movies to sitcoms (especially *Saved by the Bell* for all you 80s babies), I garnered several great examples of how to sabotage my single life. The lessons I learned are actually conventional ideas concerning singleness that were implicitly demonstrated to me through various people and media. But I've been taught that if you learn, you must teach!

So, here I am to teach the coveted knowledge on ruining your single life. I figured I would do us all a favor and pinpoint some .key principles to sabotaging our singleness. No longer do you have to hit and miss. You can nail the bull's eye every time! I dare not keep these nuggets to myself any longer, so let's take a ride and see how you, too, can learn to be *Unsuccessfully Single!*

1. A Terrible Example

One of the worst examples I've seen on how to sabotage your single life comes from my grandparents (Papa and Grandma). They celebrated nearly sixty years of wedded bliss before my grandmother passed away. They remained virgins until their wedding day. Papa wasn't exploring multiple women simultaneously while he was single. He was committed exclusively and when he dated someone, it was because he intended to marry. When it didn't work out, he respected the young lady's wishes and left her alone. After a few failed relationships, he finally found the one his heart desired. Papa never thought he would marry my grandmother. They had some of the same friends, but he never looked at her as a potential mate.

One day, my grandfather was driving his father's new car and decided to pick up some friends. While they were riding, his friends suggested, *Hey, Isaac, let's pick up Margaret Gordy* (that's my Grandma). When he arrived at her house, she politely asked if it was alright to ride with them. Of course, he agreed!

They all loaded in the car and began their ride down the streets of old Detroit. As my grandfather dropped everyone off, Margaret was his last stop. On the ride home, they were faced with some unforeseen circumstances. They got into a pretty serious car accident in his father's new car! That accident resulted in my grandmother having to go to the hospital.

She was in the hospital for a few days recovering from her injuries. Each day she was there, Papa would go and visit her. His friends would tell him, *You don't have to go and visit her every day! The accident was not your fault.* Papa responded back,

I don't have to, but I want to!

Those hospital visits would soon blossom into something much more. Eventually, they were committed to each other. He knew he wanted to marry her. Before he popped the question, he was sure to get the approval of his parents and her parents, especially her father,

Mr. Henry Berry Gordy. My grandparents grew close by accident, but they dated and married with purpose, on purpose.

Are you thinking what I'm thinking? Beautiful story? Indeed. Terrible example of how to sabotage your single life? You bet! Now, let's take their story and flip it, and I will show you how to have an *Unsuccessfully Single* life.

2. Passive and Pursued

A young man reluctantly entered into a relational situation he knew wouldn't work. From the very beginning, his lady friend was the pursuer. Daily, he received calls from her, and she showered him compliments, all of this without even having a "title".

She would tell him how great is, compliment his clothes, his hair, and pretty much everything about him. He didn't think too much of it and actually enjoyed the attention (I guess *words of affirmation* was his *love language*). Now, he wasn't one to be easily swayed by such compliments, but in a way, he began to believe his own press clippings, as they say. Knowing all too well that this was not an ideal relationship, he decided not to pursue her, but instead, just talk to her whenever she called. Well, she called virtually EVERYDAY at ANYTIME of day!

Gradually, he entertained the idea of seeing her in order to settle things a bit, but he found himself compromising on many levels just to maintain a friendship with her.

To avoid heartbreak, he decided it was best they just be friends, but she wasn't having it. He was torn between actually having feelings, filling his relational void, and the reality that she was not really the one for him. He was reminded of her pit bull grip whenever he flirted with spending time together. When he tried to pull away, she didn't let go. Honestly, he wanted to be a fair and upstanding guy by not leading along the friendship to a dead end, but passivity got the best of him.

The cycle continued. Inundated with daily phone calls, text messages, social media messages, and emails, it seemed as if the madness would never stop. All he could think was, "Stalker Alert!" This process happened a few times before he decided to completely cease contact. The compliments he once received from her replayed in his head like a scratched CD or broken record (remember those?). What was once melodious to him was now an irritating reminder of how he allowed himself to be passively pursued by someone he really didn't want. Of course, it was easier to blame her for all the trouble, but he had to assign blame to himself. He knew what he didn't want and yet flirted with the idea anyway, only to be hurt in the end.

One of those daytime judge shows was on. A couple had broken up and were at odds because of cheating and other squabbles. During the court session, the plaintiff told the judge, "I'm gorgeous and women like me." Any reasonable guy would not utter those words to you, young lady, but he sure will feel it if you begin to pursue him. Pursuing the guy inflates his ego a great deal. It makes him believe he truly *is* a hot commodity.

...

Ladies, you've heard it before: "Be independent! Go after what you want! It's your life!" That's a recipe for success for a career, dream, or passion of yours, but a recipe for disaster in a relationship. So I say, *Go for it!* When you ardently pursue a guy, it weakens his desire to pursue you. The more aggressive you are, the less work he has to do.

It removes the need for him to have backbone in the relationship when you decide to make things easy. He knows you will always call and rebound to him whenever he needs you.

So, go get him! Hand him your number and give him open invitation to call you. Invite him on dates consistently. Be completely obvious about your desire to be with him. Shower him with compliments and watch his head swell like a balloon!

As a result of this behavior, you'll become the *Go-to Friend.* You'll be the friend he goes to for a weekend lunch here, movie night there, an occasional in-depth conversation. It will be sporadic, but settle for limited time with him. Now, be cautious if he ever decides that you are not the one he desires. He'll demonstrate this by calling you on his time for a little while, and then, after getting bored with you, resting the onus of initiating contact on you.

You may have wondered, *Why doesn't he ever call or text like he used to?* He knows you're good for a weekly call. He'll suddenly find himself too busy to make time with you and will likely not tell you directly. What is a girl to do? Nag him and call him relentlessly, just as the young lady in our story did. Remind him of all the good times you all have had together. Tell him, *I'm the one for you!* He may ignore it, but those words will ring in his head. Ignore his pleas for you to move on and find someone else. He will eventually tire of you calling and texting him and simply give in, making him feel comfortable with the dysfunction of the relationship. He may very well settle for you in order to keep peace.

Now, watch out! He may try to back out of this relationship again, but repeat the process. Have you ever placed your shoes on the wrong feet? That's how this relationship will feel. If so, you have successfully sabotaged your single life. Congratulations!

3. Trumping

Language changes almost as fast as technology. Every year, new words and phrases are added to our vocabulary, expanding the sea of words around us to express ourselves. One evening, I caught an episode of one of those late-night TV shows with the hipster, custom suit-wearing comedian. As he sat in his leather swivel chair, he announced the next sketch for the night. This particular sketch was all about new slang words. Some of them were rather comical, and others were mildly inappropriate. But one word the comedic host mentioned really struck a chord with me. It's a fairly new term, so you probably won't find it on the *Urban Dictionary*. The word is *trumping*.

Trumping: agitating your girlfriend/boyfriend with constant rude remarks or behavior in an effort to make him/her break up with you. It usually causes him/her to like you more.

I couldn't help but laugh! Have you ever been trumped or trumped somebody? It is the passive-aggressive way out of a relationship. Instead of just naming our feelings and clearing the air, we act out and behave in ways that no one can figure out. Usually, the trumped party will reason the behavior and explain it away. *I know she's been having a really hard month. She doesn't really mean it. He's not his usual self. Maybe I need to be a little more considerate.*

...

Are you in a relationship and can't figure a way out? You want to save face and not look like the bad guy (or girl)? Then pull the trump card, my friends. Shift all responsibility to the other party. Why should you look like the culprit? This will keep you from having to feel like you hurt someone's feelings. After all, they'll do the dirty work.

Yeah, it could be dishonest and downright deceptive. You'll have to deal with those emotions. You could say the craziest things and engage in some outlandish behavior, and your boyfriend/girlfriend will put up a fight for some time. In those moments, just slightly turn up the trump. You want to do enough to be looked at as a jerk, but not too much to appear like a mean, unruly person. Thank you, Mr. Late-Night-TV-Show Host. You scored big with this one!

4. Ignore Family and Friends

I heard the cries of a frustrated single young woman via her social media soapbox. She said, *It doesn't matter what anyone thinks about who you are dating. It's your life!*

By conventional dating standards, which usually facilitate the growth of *Unsuccessfully Single* individuals, she is totally right! Ignore anything your close friends and family have to say about who you are dating. Your friends and family see you in ways you don't see yourself. They understand your personality, your quirks, your flaws, likes, and dislikes. They can look critically and objectively at your dating situation. Their outside view enables them to give you insight that you wouldn't have otherwise because of your close proximity to the situation. I have seen this happen a lot with horrendous results.

I'm sure you have known that lady who was dating a less-than-stellar gentleman, and all her family and friends said, *He is NO*

GOOD! She usually replies with *You're just jealous!* or *You don't know him like I know him!* Yes, keep that attitude, sister! Your family and friends are not jealous. You are just farsighted and securing your first-class ticket to a frustrating single life and a potentially disastrous marriage.

The more you ignore the sound counsel of friends and family, the more brainwashed you'll become. You will think everyone is crazy except the person you are dating.

Another case study

Jim had been dating a young lady for all of two weeks. Emotions got high rather quickly, and the relationship was getting pretty serious. He was already thinking about wedding rings and resolved early on that this was the girl he wanted to marry. Jim even got some seemingly divine words from a mentor saying, *She is your wife!*

Convinced of these words and his emotions, Jim thought it was time to tell Dad. Before the conversation, Jim shared with his girlfriend that he would talk to his dad about their relationship. This strategy was to legitimize their relationship and get his dad's approval. That time for conversing finally came. There Jim sat at the table, with his dad on the opposite end fiddling with papers. With a nervous gulp in his throat, Jim started the conversation rather forthrightly.

Jim: *Dad, I think I've found the one!*

(Silence...for what seemed like an eternity)

Dad: *You found the one for what?*

Jim: *Well...the one to marry.*

Dad: *Oh. Do you go on dates?*

(More silence, thumb twiddling, and paper fiddling)

This question caught Jim by surprise as he realized that they hadn't really been anywhere alone. He made up an answer.

Jim: *Um...yeah, we hang out and go places.*

*This was true technically, but the real dating hadn't happened. It had only been two weeks!

Dad: *Well...there's no rush. We'll be praying.*

And pray he did! The relationship ended as quickly as it started. Jim usually kept his relationship life secret from his parents (a concept we will deal with in the next chapter). He generally neglected to ask for their advice before getting involved with someone.

A few years later, Jim's dad asked, *How are things between you and the young lady?* Jim was somewhat surprised by the question because it had been so long since his relationship ended. After telling his dad that it didn't work out, his father replied, *Oh. I knew she wasn't the one for you.* Of course, Jim was somewhat puzzled at his father's words and wondered why his dad didn't say something three years prior. Jim's dad gave an interesting response, *You already had your mind made up about her. So I chose not to say anything.*

Ouch!

When you tell your friends and family that you have already made up your mind about someone or that *God told me*, what else can they say? Any contrary words concerning your decision can cause rifts and dissension since we generally desire someone's affirmation more than their criticism. Imagine what would have happened if Jim ignored his father's counsel. What if he got into a rush and just did what felt right?

5. Shhh! It's a Secret

The longer you keep your dating life a secret, the better your chances of getting deeper and deeper involved with someone who is not for you. You are well on your way to sabotaging your singleness. Good job!

Jim broke one of our sabotaging rules: he did not keep his dating life a secret. His openness with his dad allowed another voice of reason into his dating relationship. Keeping your dating life a secret will blind you to the warning signs and red flags others may see. Play it risky and enter the relationship without previous counsel. If you hide as much as you can, and it turns out to be a bad relationship, you can get deeper entangled in an emotional and relational trap.

Why keep your relationships a secret from those closest to you?

Lack of Accountability

With no one around to ask you questions and check up on you, you are bound to make a bad decision or two concerning your relationship. With zero accountability, you are prone to say and do things that may prove harmful to you and the one you are dating. You will be able to have your fun, and no one will rain on your good time.

To Avoid Rejection

Oftentimes, we know that if we tell someone what is happening with our dating relationships, we might be met with unfavorable critiques and lack of support. Avoid the potential rejection from friends and family concerning your relationship, and you can maintain a false sense of support.

Remember, if no one knows you're dating, the better your chances of making a really bad decision concerning your dating and marital future, especially if your partner is questionable.

6. "It's Our Anniversary!" Not really

Babe! We've been dating for five years! Let's celebrate!

Here is a not-so-subtle sabotaging mechanism: make a big deal out of your dating anniversaries. Show the world and your boyfriend/girlfriend that it is your *pseudo* commitment to each other that counts and not a wedding ring and marriage license. The more emphasis you place on your dating anniversaries, the more attention is drawn away from the overarching goal: marriage.

Keep your partner so enthralled that you all have been dating for three years, four years, five years and beyond that marriage becomes a secondary issue. There are some who have been dating 15 to 20 years strong, have children together, and have never tied the knot. They enjoy all the intimacy without the security of commitment. You can be next...if you want to sabotage your single life.

Getting married demonstrates that next level of true, wholehearted commitment. On the contrary, emphasis on the dating alone allows you to *have your cake and eat it, too.* Here's the deal, if you're getting everything you could possibly want anyway—time, affection, love, intimacy—why go all the way and get married? Dating to marry is pretty old school and will hamper your progress of sabotaging your single life (Remember my grandparents)!

7. Just Friends…Sorta

While in college, just for fun, we made up a continuum for dating relationships.

The Relationship Continuum

Close Friends	Unofficially Talking	Committed Relationship

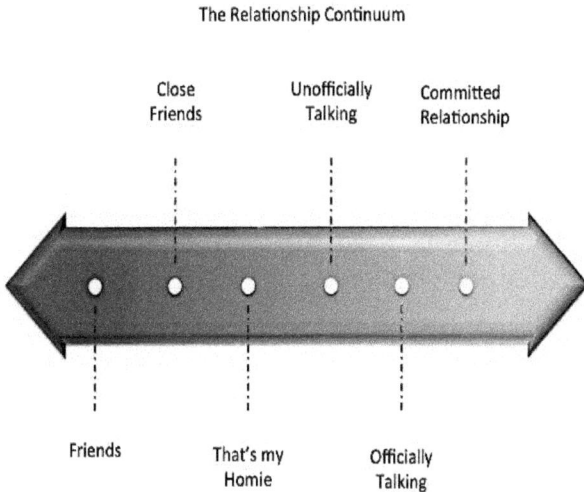

Friends	That's my Homie	Officially Talking

We recognized that there were these gray areas in relationships that don't have a name, yet they are very real relational areas. These areas of complexity have often been overlooked and have become sources of confusion and tension. One popular social media site offers three relational labels: Single,

Married, and *It's Complicated.* Without clearly defined relationships, anything goes. With no rules and boundaries, people will inevitably get hurt. That's the joy of *It's Complicated.* One person will think there is more to the friendship (right of the continuum) while the other is still in the *friend zone* (left of the continuum). One will be left to wonder if his/her friend is *more than just a friend* or may ask, *Will we ever get together/married?*

Girls, if you desire to further complicate your relationship, never ask the guy what his intentions are for you. Do not make him step up to the plate and *man up* to his responsibility to pursue. It may challenge him, expose his true motives, and may even make him stop dating you. Is that what you really want? Absolutely not!

Guys, keep your mouth closed about your future together and remain as ambiguous as possible. No need to make any lasting commitments. It is highly probable that she will be too naive to ask you outright about your intentions and spend months, even years, tagging along in a dating relationship. It will weigh emotionally on her, and she could be another heartbreak on your watch because of your no-strings-attached mentality. The sabotage is in full effect!

Some people are in what one of my old friends called a *rela-friendship* (pronounced re-lay-friendship). It's that awkward, cloudy, undefined area when you know you're more than friends, but you never put a name or purpose to what you're doing relationally. If you remember these points—don't ask questions, don't have the hard conversations, and don't draw clear-cut lines to define the relationship—you can also arrive at that ambiguous relational area. Just keep floating like a sailboat, allowing the friendship to coast in the wind aimlessly.

8. Ride the Close Bus

Carl was involved in a *rela-friendship*. He and his lady friend, Ashley, were dating for some time but never made anything official. Ashley wondered why Carl didn't make a move toward a commitment, but she hesitated to ask. After several months of talking, getting to know each other, and hanging out, Ashley finally broke the *Unsuccessfully Single* rule and asked Carl a pointed question:

"Carl, are you *close-busing* me?"

Clearly confused by her question, Carl replied,

"*Close-busing?* What do you mean?"

Ashley went on to explain the concept of *close-busing*. It goes something like this: Let's say there's a destination you want to arrive at and there are two buses on the route that you can take. Bus 1 drops you off right in front of your destination, and Bus 2 drops you off about 15 minutes walking distance away. You're in a rush to get to your destination and Bus 1 is running slower than usual. So, in your haste, you decide to board Bus 2 when it comes. Bus 2 will get you into the vicinity of your destination, but it actually won't get you there. After her explanation, she asked again,

"Carl, are you *close-busing* me?"

Carl was pricked to his heart and at a loss for words. He knew exactly what was in his heart but was too timid to communicate it. He indeed was riding the *close bus*. He did not give her the respect she deserved by settling beneath his standards.

Sometimes, relationships are like that. We *close-bus* people who really aren't what we are looking for. They have some qualities we like and admire, but they don't quite hit the mark. So, instead of waiting for the one that fits our needs (and ultimately the one whose needs we fit), we ride the close bus. We settle for the instant instead of waiting for what we truly desire, the person who truly helps us arrive at that place of fulfillment. The close bus has passengers such as Mr. Almost But Not Quite and Sister Kinda But Not Really. Those on the close bus aren't the worst picks or not even bad picks, but they simply don't fulfill all that you want in a mate. Those on the close bus are the people we decide to settle for because we refuse to wait. Ride the close bus for the ultimate relationship-settling experience. It will leave you underwhelmed and constantly asking, *What if I had waited?*

9. The Mosaic Mate

It is highly probable that dating a person exclusively with the intention to marry will minimize your chances of emotional and relational turmoil. It will keep you from investing time, energy, and money in people you know you are not going to marry. However, let us not forget our objective: to sabotage our single lives, not salvage them.

The more people you get emotionally involved with, the better. This will help you compare your current dating partner to others to see if that person measures up. Since we all know there are no perfect people or mates, having multiple people in your emotional space and dating space will most likely lead you to construct the *Mosaic Mate.* The Mosaic Mate is the ideal person you create by weaving together a conglomeration of the traits you like most from each candidate you are dating. You like Jim's personality, Carl's laughter, and John's spirituality. All three give you the perfect guy, but neither of them individually possesses all you want. Toya's looks, Jane's quietness, Ashley's passion, and Brittany's affirmation of you all suit your fancy, but neither one really hits it out of the park. Having multiple options at your disposal makes the perfect person figuratively but will certainly leave you disappointed, since such imagined persons do not exist. Maintaining these rela-friendships will prove to be difficult. All these gray areas will make for cloudy days in your relational life. The sober way would be to wait, but the *Unsuccessfully Single* way is to doubt that you will ever find such a great person and build a Mosaic Mate. However, be cautioned. You might be a piece in someone else's Mosaic Mate!

10. Practice Being Married

Another surefire way to sabotage your single life, and possibly the most obvious, is to act married while you're single. Enjoy the intimacy and privileges of marriage without ever committing.

Living together before you are married will give you an inaccurate assessment of what it will be like to be married, increasing your chances of not only an *Unsuccessfully Single* life, but also an unsuccessfully married life (but that's another book for another time).

Ask those who have lived together before they were married. They'll be sure to tell you the myriad of surprises and unexpected findings they encountered once tying the knot—findings that didn't show up when they lived together before getting married. Everyone likes surprises.

The practice of being married will undoubtedly increase temptation. Let's face it;

no one likes the nag of temptation. Living with your partner or even spending unhealthy amounts of private time with them will bring temptation like you've never known. The nag of sexual temptation will be increased and you'll tire of fighting off the urge. Now, your conscience will be bothered when you *slip up* a few times, but don't worry. The more you engage in temptation, your radar will become dimmer and dimmer. Your conscience will grow dull and become so seared that you'll no longer even recognize you are doing wrong. And this is good for the sabotaging process.

Don't let anything stop you from engaging in temptation. It's good! Now you will notice some guilty feelings as you initially indulge your savory, lustful desires. But no need to worry. It gets easier to ignore over time.

11. Leave Your Thoughts Untamed

I spent some time on the golf course, and it was a sight to see. The grass was so well manicured. There wasn't a weed anywhere! The turf was laid out so nicely that I couldn't tell it wasn't real grass. It was a utopia of greenery. I have also seen some unsavory lawns. Weeds, patches, and brown grass abound with overgrown grass and not a lawnmower in sight.

Do you have both pictures in your head yet? The latter is where we are headed—an untamed thought life. This *Unsuccessfully Single* method is possibly the easiest to employ because of how few individuals are needed to pull it off. All that is needed for this one is you since you are with yourself everywhere you go. Letting your thoughts go wild creates unrealistic fantasies and expectations for yourself and for others you would desire to consider for a mate. Indulge in the latest magazines with airbrushed humans on the pages and movies with fanatical romantic scenarios and steamy passion.

Photo-shopped abdomens, eyebrows, and flawless, color-corrected skin can be your delight. Surreal hook ups, cinematic lighting, and constant soundtracks of sultry strings, warmth sounds, and nature will create the ultimate backdrop for thoughts to go wild. Indulging in surrealism will affect relationships with real people as you seek to have others live up to the standard you've created in your mind. You'll never find that digitally altered beauty or knight in real life, which makes this one of the most frustrating and successful methods for infecting your singleness.

So you're not one for mags and movies? That's cool. There's something for you, too! Replaying the inappropriateness of your past relationships in your mind is another way to let your mind go wild and untamed. This may seem like a safer route to go, since no one else will be involved, but it will affect you emotionally and relationally, just as good as movies and magazines can.

Replaying the "good times" from your past relationships will seem to help you in your lonely times. A mental pursuit of those moments may take the edge off of the frustration of being single temporarily, but will ultimately leave you unsatisfied, digging a deeper hole in your heart. You will repeat these thoughts daily as needed since the withdrawal will become stronger at times. Try to avoid sober thoughts, positive self-talk, and any sort of spiritual words like Scriptures or inspirational quotes. Those methods serve to tame your thought life and will hinder your intoxication via uncontrolled thoughts.

12. Drop Your Standards

Remember when you were a teen and you had a laundry list of what you wanted in a mate? You might have listed 1) good hair, 2) supermodel/beach-body physique, 3) no kids, 4) cooks and cleans (for the fellas), and 5) a whole lotta money (for the ladies)!

Then, when you hit your mid-twenties, your list got a little shorter: 1) cute face, 2) a kid is ok, 3) religious, and 4) a really good job (for the ladies).

And finally, when you hit the thirties and beyond, your list became 1) grand-kids are ok, 2) like the opposite sex, 3) at least a job, and 4) religious is optional.

As we get older, some things on our list began to fade out. What was once very important becomes less important or non-essential. This is highly necessary in order to achieve future relational complications. No matter what you do, be sure to compromise on your deal breakers. If it really matters to you, tell yourself that you're the only one out there who meets your standards. Settling is the order of the day!

I knew a good Christian guy who planned to date a good Muslim girl. He told me, *Like spokes on a bicycle wheel going to the center, all roads lead to God. Marrying her will mix things up at my church.* He is right about one thing; he will be mixed up! To his credit, his heart is in the right place—date someone with completely different spiritual beliefs so that things can be *mixed up*. But he is confused about the true results.

Despite his confusion about what is really happening, he is actually on the road to sabotaging his singleness and his future marriage. He is in for some serious debates, confusion, and isolation. They won't see eye-to-eye, will not worship together, and will find out that they have more differences than things in common. Good job, kiddo!

They say that opposites attract just like magnets. Date someone who is nothing like you. It will seem very novel and fun at first. This is really good bait that will lead to rifts along the way. She wants tons of kids, and you want one. She is into church and does everything, but you are more of a bench warmer. You are a gym nut, but he hates working out. You like to talk, but he hates to listen. When you see that you two are quite different, force yourself to make it work because who knows if you'll ever be able to find who you really want?

Ignore all warning signs. Urge her to do what you want to make you happy, and make her feel bad if she doesn't. Seek out ways to change him and make him into the guy you really desire. If he doesn't change, nag him and cry! This is a great way to manipulate him to go along with your program. Dropping your standards will put you in an uphill battle, trying to change a person to fit your desires. It'll be like trying to force that one puzzle piece into an area it wasn't designed for. It may look like it fits, but it doesn't match the rest of the picture.

13. Get Obsessed with Marriage

Wedding shows, magazines, blogs—there is enough media available out there for you to obsess about getting married. Are you one of those girls who has been planning out your wedding day since you were 12 years old? Great! Continue to flood every moment of your single life with thoughts of marriage. I would encourage you to begin planning your wedding now, without a potential mate in sight. Cut out the magazine clips and make your wedding vision board. Go to every wedding you can and keep visualizing yourself going down the aisle. Immerse every moment of your single life in deep thoughts of marriage so you can begin to loathe being single and forget that singleness is actually a gift.

Sarah is the scrapbook queen! Amongst her scrapbooking projects was a wedding board. Knocking on thirty's door, she felt her clock ticking and strongly desired to get married. On her wall hung a wedding poster of a famous couple with her face pasted over the celebrity's face. Every day, evening and morning, she had thoughts of marriage on her mind.

Her lucky day finally came! A guy expressed interest. He was a clean-cut, educated fellow. They dated, and she brought up marriage almost immediately. Things moved quickly as Sarah reminded him constantly about her desire to get married. She bypassed the family talks, the premarital counseling, and sage advice. She had already made up her mind and wanted no one to stand in her way.

After a few months, Sarah and her beau tied the knot! Her wedding dreams were coming to life! The colors, the cake, the venue, the honeymoon were all she planned for and dreamed of. There was just one small problem. In planning for the wedding day, Sarah and her now husband didn't take time to adequately plan the marriage. She began to realize that there were dreams and goals she now wanted to accomplish that she had to put on hold.

Her husband experienced the same thing. They began to discover they both had very different personal values, and this caused a great deal of clashing in their marriage. They both missed out on some serious personal development and exploration of each other's lives while they were dating because of the allure of marriage.

Now, this hypothetical story serves to support a point. The obsession with marriage while you are single helps to blunt your senses concerning the life you live currently. This obsession helps you to see your single years as merely transitional and not a time to make any real progress. As a result, you will miss out on prime years of being single. Then, when you finally get married (if you ever do), you will wish you had done more with your life while you were single.

There are many singles who obsess about being married, only to become married people who obsess about being single. Buy into the school of thought that being single means you're incomplete, lacking, and less than. This will help increase your desperation and potentially set you up to settle for whomever comes your way. Stay thirsty, ladies and gents.

14. Media Stalk Your Ex

Hmm, I wonder what she's up to...

That's where it begins. A little curiosity about your ex goes a long way. With scores of social networks at your fingertips, it is quite easy to see what's happening in the life of your ex. From posts, pictures, and live video feeds to stories and snapshots of your life on the latest social media platforms, the resources for checking on your ex abound. However, be alert! Some social media platforms are not good for maintaining your secrecy.

The cool thing about media stalking is that your ex only posts what looks the best, is most intriguing, or whatever helps to shape the reality he or she wants. So what you're watching is not *real*, but will inscribe an image on your mind that you will consider real. Media stalking your ex (or even someone you desire) helps to create a pseudo-connection. It will likely create a deeper longing in your heart for them and stall the healing process from your failed relationship.

Any potential person who comes your way, you will miss out on, or at worst, constantly compare that person to the cropped and edited ex your heart believes is real. My suggestion is to browse without a trace if you desire to just keep it your secret. Become a bonafide lurker. No likes, no comments, no retweets, no reposts. The media stalking will be like a cotton candy treat—sweet and delightful, but dissolved as soon as you begin to taste it.

You'll urge for real-life interaction, but because you know you won't get it, the stalking can continue. This will become a perpetual cycle that will assist in filling your time of singleness with pipe dreams that will never materialize. It will make you utterly hate being single and create a relational world that does not exist. Remember the *Mosaic Mate*?

She blocked me!

So your ex blocked you on social media? No problemo! You can sink to a new low and use your friend's media devices to check your ex's profile. Want to get even nosier? Start checking the profile of your ex's new romantic interest. You will feel so empty after all this snooping, decrease your own self-image, and (you guessed it) ruin your single life. You can thank me later. But beware! When you think no one knows, somebody is probably hip to your secret.

A little curiosity is all it takes to pull you into the black hole of media stalking. It's a dark and lonely place—the perfect place for the *Unsuccessfully Single.*

15. Let Go of Your Dreams

She's *that* girl. The one every guy always asks, *Is she single?* She's the one that gets voted *Most Beautiful* and *Most likely to Succeed.* She is the one YOU want. And of course, someone else has her. But something grips you. Something inside says, *Dude, this is it! This is the one!* No other relationship seems to work. No other person seems to fit. You're sick of the mosaic mate.

And so, you go for it! You launch out and spill your guts to THE Girl. And she gives you those words that no guy ever wants to hear under any circumstances, *Aww, that's so sweet, bro. But I'm involved.* Now, you could handle her saying she's involved. You can even handle *aww* because at least she's flattered, but *Bro?* Your heart sinks as you are placed in the **BrO-Zone Layer**. What's a guy to do?

Give up, of course. *But what about the confirmations I had? The chemistry? And she's still not married!* Yeah, lose hope, man. Squelch that dream. Why?

It's safer. At least you know you can go after someone who will be a shoe-in. You know a girl who likes you already. She's just waiting for you to make a move, so make it. So you give up hope. You let go of the girl of your dreams to a guy who really doesn't know her worth. And everyday you ask yourself, *What if?* You look in the face of the one you chose and you loathe your choice. Poor guy. She doesn't even know that she was a plan B, a rebound, a just-in-case. Oh, but it gets better. You were actually *her* rebound. She had her hopes set on someone else, too.

Had you gone for it and waited out, you probably would have achieved your heart's desire. But it's so much risk involved. I mean, she already turned you down once. Are you really going to try again? You're getting older everyday before you know it, you'll be THIRTY YEARS OLD AND *Unsuccessfully Single*. You'll be a grandpa. Do away with waiting for the person of your dreams. Live in the real world. The real deal is that it's too much of a risk. Play it safe and stay in the shallow end.

16. Watch for the Trap!

There will be people who come along and try to give you good advice on being single. They will say silly things like *Wait until you are married to have sex*, or *Run away from the slightest hint of sexual temptation. Enjoy being single! Live it up now!* Yada yada.

I'm not sure if I could be any more blunt than this, but DON'T listen to them! They want what's best for you, and they want you to have a successful single life and happy married life. But that is counter-cultural; that is going against the grain. Not cool! You will contrast with the majority of Hollywood images.

You will look like an oddball amongst your peers. You will defy the conventional wisdom in television, movies, magazines, and fairytale films. But remember your mission: sabotage your single life. If you stay true to the teachings in this book, you'll be well on your way. I'm sure most of you are already there. *Overachievers!*

Appendix A: Kissing the Night Away!

Do you remember the first time you saw a fairytale movie? The damsel in distress is pursued and rescued by some daring, adventurous man. Lonely and afraid, she flails her arms helplessly, as he battles the villain, defeating him and snatching his beauty into his arms. But it's not over until he seals the deal with a classic closed-mouth kiss!

Many of the animated movies we watched during childhood carried similar story lines and were ingrained in our young minds. Amidst the varying storylines and plots, one scene is common throughout all of these films: the kissing scene—Aladdin and Jasmine's date with concluding kiss, Tarzan and Jane's tumbling kiss on the seashore, Hercules movie-ending kiss with a mortal. *Pucker up!*

A kiss is a common part of our culture. We kiss our babies, our parents, our siblings, and our friends. There is a kiss that is cordial and appropriate for greeting. It communicates friendship and closeness. But a kiss can communicate so much more.

There is a story in the Bible about a beautiful woman named Rebekah who was married to a wealthy man named Isaac. Rebekah was so beautiful that Isaac thought the men where they lived would kill him so they could marry her. To save his own head (and potentially lose his beautiful wife), he lied and told people that Rebekah was his sister. One day, the king was looking out his window and saw Isaac interacting with his wife in a way that married couples do. The king drew this conclusion and said, "Without a doubt, she is your wife! Why did you say she was your sister?" (Genesis 26:7-11).

I want to highlight the fact that Isaac engaged in a physical manner with Rebekah that was regarded as appropriate for married individuals. Whatever the interaction, it was deemed acceptable for a married couple, and yet inappropriate for a sibling relationship. I can only think of two public interactions that would be "acceptable" for married couples, but perhaps even questionable for public display, depending on how far it goes: kissing and touching. For now, let's just say it was kissing.

There is a kiss that says, *You are my family/friend*, and then there's a kiss that says, *You are my spouse.* Without splitting hairs about kissing, let's just put it like this: a this-is-not-my-sister kiss is more than just a kiss.

I think most of us have longed for the first kiss. We saw it in most of our childhood movies and all around us. I can remember wondering what a kiss would be like. That was my relational goal as a teenager—to kiss a girl. And then, one day, it happened! It seemed surreal. After it happened, it felt like it didn't really happen.

Am I dreaming? Did this really just happen? The kiss stirred something in me— feelings I had never felt, desires I didn't know I had, so many emotions, and the desire to do it again with no strings attached. So that became the goal—link up with a girl just so I could kiss her. Little do some people recognize the emotional implications that come with *married* kissing when they're single. This ignorance works to their disadvantage as it delicately weaves a web of emotions and feelings that are best reserved for marriage.

I heard a great philosopher say (who am I kidding, it was probably from some one's Facebook status or a random conversation) that kissing is *an upward persuasion for a downward invasion.* Now, I won't be naïve and say that kissing is going to lead to sex, but I know one thing for sure, kissing leaves a desire for more. Kissing can lead to, obviously, more kissing, more time with a person, and for most, more physical interaction. Passionate kissing arouses in a way that's not meant to be turned off. This poses a great hindrance for thriving as a single person, as it heightens emotions and desires that can prove difficult to control.

For girls, usually the emotions that come from kissing lead to a desire for commitment. Out of context, kissing could become a sabotaging element during your single life. Consider this, how many people have you kissed that you aren't married to or that married someone else? You could find yourself wrapped up with some one's future spouse, or even worse, someone could be tampering with your future spouse!

So, why turn the emotional switch on and off? Try to save that kiss for the wedding day. It'll mean so much more, and you'll thank yourself for reserving those emotions and actions until the right time.

Appendix B: Real Talk

You made it through the book! Enough of the satire. Let's talk straight and just keep it real. All of this dating talk can sometimes seem like an impossible list of *do's* and *don'ts.* And as much as I would like to tell you that all of this is easy, sometimes it is downright difficult. There are times when we know what's right and do the exact opposite. Feeling like a hypocrite isn't fun, but it reveals something. If you feel bad for not keeping it together, it shows your desire to actually do what's right concerning the people you will form relationships with. And we *should* desire to have the person's best interests in mind.

So, what's the simple way to keep all of this in balance? Should one tote this little book around and memorize the points so they can maintain a(an) (Un)successfully Single life? Honestly, I think the easiest way to hold all of these principles together is simply to treat people the way you would want to be treated.

I have twin sisters whom I love dearly. They have grown into beautiful young ladies. I know that one day they will have relationships and husbands of their own. When I see them, I think about how I would want someone to treat them. I want a young man to have the utmost respect for my sisters in every way. If he's bored and just wants to pass time, I want him to stay far away. If he pursues and figures out that this isn't what he wants, I want him to be honest enough to end the relationship. If he hasn't put a ring on the finger and made it official, I want him to wait until the wedding day to take the plunge.

When I desire this for my sisters, I have to ask myself, *Am I treating other young ladies this way? Would I want a guy like me to date my sisters?* This is something I think about often. Those thoughts, along with my love for God and the desire to treat others the way I want to be treated, serve to keep me in check.

Though I have penned these pages, the principles in this book are something that I want to constantly strive for and live up to (of course, the opposite thereof). We may not get it right all the time, but do know that you can get it right and have a successful single life and maintain healthy, meaningful relationships.

Kellen serves as the lead pastor of Pentecostal Temple Church Of God in Christ in Inkster, MI. Along with pastoral ministry and authorship, Kellen is a professional musician, songwriter, music producer, and adjunct instructor at Ashland Theological Seminary (Detroit Campus). Kellen is a sought-after speaker with local, national, and international reach. To find out more about *Unsuccessfully Single* seminars and speaking engagements, or to book Kellen for your next event, please visit KellenBrooks.com.

www.ingramcontent.com/pod-product-compliance
Lightning Source LLC
Chambersburg PA
CBHW071418040426
42445CB00012BA/1209